The Big Day!
A New Baby Arrives

Nicola Barber

PowerKiDS press.

New York

Published in 2009 by The Rosen Publishing Group Inc.
29 East 21st Street, New York, NY 10010

First Edition

Editor: Camilla Lloyd
Designer: Elaine Wilkinson
Picture Researcher: Kathy Lockley

Library of Congress Cataloging-in-Publication Data

Barber, Nicola.
  A new baby arrives / Nicola Barber. — 1st ed.
     p. cm. — (The big day!)
  Includes bibliographical references and index.
  ISBN 978-1-4358-2842-1 (library binding: alk. paper)
  ISBN 978-1-4358-2898-8 (paperback)
  ISBN 978-1-4358-2902-2 (6-pack)
  1. Newborn infants—Juvenile literature. 2. Brothers and sisters—Juvenile literature.
  3. Family—Juvenile literature. I. Title.
  HQ774.B332 2009
  306.875'3—dc22

                                   2008026223

Manufactured in China

Picture Acknowledgments: The author and publisher would like to thank the following for their
pictures to be reproduced in this publication: Cover photograph: Larry Williams/zefa/Corbis;
Chuck Savage/Corbis: 17; CuboImages srl/Alamy Images: 19; David Oliver/Stone/Getty Images:
1, 11; Jenny Acheson/Riser/Getty Images: 13; John James/Alamy Images: 10, 24; Jose Luis Pelaez,
Inc/Corbis: 15; Larry Williams/zefa/Corbis: 16; Michael Keller/Corbis: 12; Owen Franken/Corbis:
14, 21; Patrick Lacroix/The Image Bank/Getty Images: 9; Phillipe Lissac/Godong/Corbis: 18; Ross
Whitaker/The Image Bank/Getty Images: 20; Sally & Richard Greenhill/Alamy Images: 6; Stewart
Cohen/Blend Images/Getty Images: 7; Superstudio/Iconica/Getty Images: 5; Tim
Brown/Stone/Getty Images: 8.

Contents

Mom is having a baby

Your Mom is having a baby. The baby has been growing inside your Mom for almost nine months.

What will the new baby be like?

Now Mom's tummy is big, and sometimes
you can feel the baby moving around inside.
Soon it will be time for the baby to be born.

 # Getting ready

It's fun to help your Mom and Dad get everything ready for the new baby.

You can help to choose the decorations for the baby's room.

You can buy some toys for the new baby
to play with.

Meeting the baby

When it's time for the baby to be born, your Mom will probably go to the hospital.

Soon, you can go to meet your new brother or sister. What is it like holding the baby for the first time?

Welcoming the baby

Sometimes, if a baby is born early, he or she may stay in the hospital for a little while.

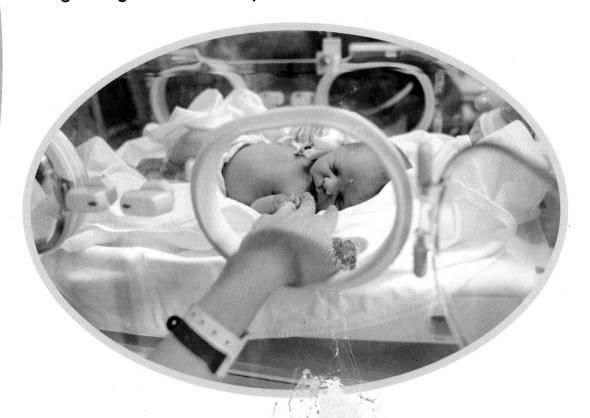

Your Mom will help to look after the baby in the hospital.

Usually, your Mom and the baby will come home after a few days. It's fun to have a new brother or sister at home. But babies can make a lot of noise!

Sharing

It probably feels different at home with the new baby. Mom and Dad are often busy. But you can still have special family times together.

12

While Dad looks after the baby, Mom might take you to the library or for a bike ride.

Helping with the baby

You can help Mom and Dad to take care of the baby. You might be able to feed the baby, or change the baby's diaper.

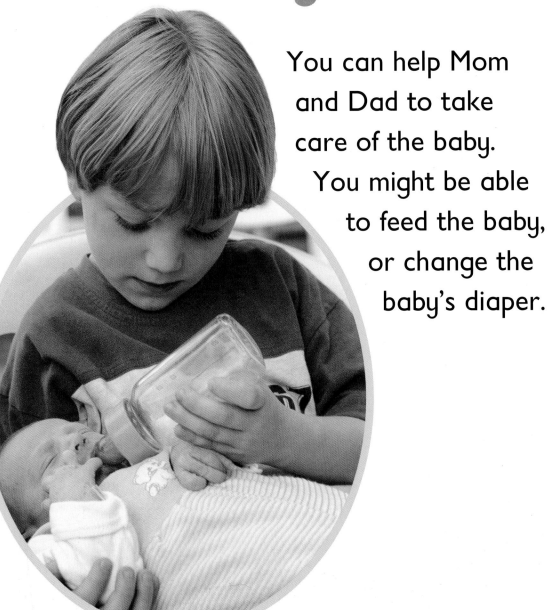

You can enjoy the peace and quiet when
the baby is asleep!

Bath time

Bath time is fun with the new baby.
The baby has a special small bath.

You can help to wash the baby,
and play with the bath toys.

After a bath,
it is often time for
the baby to go to sleep.

 # Naming the baby

Your family might have a special ceremony to welcome the new baby.

This baby is being named in a Hindu ceremony, twelve days after her birth.

This baby is having water poured over her head at her baptism. This is a Christian ceremony, when the baby is named and welcomed into the Christian religion.

First birthday

Babies grow up and change very quickly. Soon, your baby brother or sister will be sitting up and crawling around.

You will always remember the day
when your brother or sister was born—
because this is their birthday.

Happy first birthday!

Baby words

If you are writing about your new baby brother or sister, these are some of the words you might need to use.

Baptism

Diaper

Bath time

Feed

Birthday

Hospital

Brother

Sister

Ceremony

Sleep

Crawling

Toy

Further information

Books

Hi New Baby!
by Robie H Harris (Topeka Bindery, 2003)

The New Baby (Usborne First Experiences)
by Anne Civardi (Usborne Books, 2005)

The New Baby (Topsy and Tim Storybooks)
by Jean and Gareth Adamson (Ladybird Books, 2003)

What to Expect When the New Baby Comes Home
by Heidi Murkoff (Harper Festival, 2001)

Web Sites

Due to the changing nature of Internet links, PowerKids Press has developed an online list of Web sites related to the subject of this book. This site is updated regularly. Please use this link to access this list:

www.powerkidslinks.com/bd/newbaby

Index